The Ultimate Pub Quiz Book 2025 - Perfect for Pub Nights and Parties

Mark Hope

ISBN: 9798346441588

Cover design by: Elegant Impressions

Table of Contents

Chapter 1: General Knowledge

1. What is the capital city of Wales?
2. In which year did the UK officially leave the European Union?
3. What is the chemical symbol for gold?
4. Who was the first woman to become Prime Minister of the UK?
5. In which UK city would you find the Shard?
6. What is the national animal of Scotland?
7. Which author wrote *Pride and Prejudice*?
8. What is the tallest mountain in the UK?
9. How many time zones does Russia have?
10. What is the name of the currency used in Japan?
11. Who painted the Sistine Chapel ceiling?
12. What is the smallest country in the world by area?
13. How many continents are there on Earth?
14. What is the largest island in the world?
15. Which ocean is the largest by area?
16. What is the name of the longest river in South America?
17. Who invented the telephone?
18. Which planet is known as the Morning Star?
19. What is the hardest natural substance on Earth?
20. How many sides does a hexagon have?

21. What is the capital of Australia?
22. Who wrote the play *Romeo and Juliet*?
23. In which year did World War I begin?
24. What is the main ingredient in a traditional English trifle?
25. Which city hosted the first modern Olympic Games?
26. What is the speed of light?
27. Who was the first British astronaut in space?
28. What is the largest mammal in the world?
29. Which two countries share the longest international border?
30. What is the name of the Queen's official London residence?
31. Who discovered penicillin?
32. Which famous shipwreck was discovered in 1985?
33. What is the longest bone in the human body?
34. Which animal is known as the King of the Jungle?
35. What is the chemical formula for table salt?
36. Who was the Greek god of the sea?
37. How many squares are there on a standard chessboard?
38. What is the national sport of Japan?
39. Which musical instrument has 88 keys?

40. What year did the UK switch to the decimal system?
41. Who directed the film *Jurassic Park*?
42. What is the smallest unit of life?
43. Which is the only planet not named after a god?
44. In which country would you find the ancient city of Petra?
45. Who wrote the novel *Moby Dick*?
46. What is the largest desert in the world?
47. Which bird is known for its colourful, fan-shaped tail?
48. What was the first animal to be sent into space?
49. What is the official language of Brazil?
50. Who was the first person to win two Nobel Prizes?

Chapter 1: Answers

1. Cardiff
2. 2020
3. Au
4. Margaret Thatcher
5. London
6. Unicorn
7. Jane Austen
8. Ben Nevis
9. 11
10. Yen
11. Michelangelo
12. Vatican City
13. 7
14. Greenland
15. Pacific Ocean
16. Amazon River
17. Alexander Graham Bell
18. Venus
19. Diamond
20. 6
21. Canberra
22. William Shakespeare
23. 1914
24. Custard, fruit, and sponge cake
25. Athens, Greece
26. 299,792,458 meters per second
27. Helen Sharman

28.Blue whale
29.Canada and the USA
30.Buckingham Palace
31.Alexander Fleming
32.Titanic
33.Femur
34.Lion
35.NaCl
36.Poseidon
37.64
38.Sumo wrestling
39.Piano
40.1971
41.Steven Spielberg
42.Cell
43.Earth
44.Jordan
45.Herman Melville
46.Sahara Desert
47.Peacock
48.Laika the dog
49.Portuguese
50.Marie Curie

Chapter 2: History

1. Who was the longest-reigning monarch in British history?
2. In which year did the Battle of Hastings take place?
3. Who was the Prime Minister of the UK during World War II?
4. What was the name of the ship that famously sank after hitting an iceberg in 1912?
5. Which ancient civilisation built the pyramids?
6. Who was Henry VIII's first wife?
7. What year did the Berlin Wall fall?
8. Which English king was defeated at the Battle of Bosworth Field in 1485?
9. Who was the first President of the United States?
10. What year did women get the right to vote in the UK?
11. Which explorer discovered America in 1492?
12. What was the name of the first successful English colony in America?
13. In which year did the Great Fire of London occur?
14. Who was the first emperor of Rome?

15. What was the main cause of the Hundred Years' War?
16. Who led the Russian Revolution in 1917?
17. Which queen's reign was known as the Victorian era?
18. What was the name of the first man-made satellite launched into space?
19. Who was the British monarch during World War I?
20. In which year did the Titanic make its fateful maiden voyage?
21. Who was known as the "Iron Lady" of British politics?
22. What was the name of Alexander the Great's famous horse?
23. Which empire was known for its gladiatorial games?
24. What was the original name of New York City?
25. Who was the first female pharaoh of ancient Egypt?
26. Which battle ended Napoleon's rule in Europe?
27. Who invented the printing press?
28. What was the main weapon used by soldiers in World War I?
29. Which US state was the last to join the union?

30. What year did the Cuban Missile Crisis occur?
31. Who was the first Black President of South Africa?
32. Which medieval document limited the power of the English king?
33. Who was assassinated on April 14, 1865?
34. What year did the Wright brothers make their first flight?
35. Which ancient city was buried by the eruption of Mount Vesuvius?
36. Who was the ruler of the Soviet Union during World War II?
37. What was the primary language of the Roman Empire?
38. In which year did the Berlin Wall fall?
39. What was the name of the first space mission to land on the Moon?
40. Who was the British monarch during the American Revolution?
41. Which famous queen was married to Julius Caesar and Mark Antony?
42. What is the name of the ship that brought the Pilgrims to America in 1620?
43. Who was the first female Prime Minister of India?
44. Which British explorer was the first to reach the South Pole?

45. What year did the Spanish Armada attempt
    to invade England?
46. Who was the first person to circumnavigate
    the globe?
47. What year did the Euro currency come into
    use?
48. What was the largest contiguous empire in
    history?
49. Which war is often referred to as "The
    Great War"?
50. Who was known as the "Sun King" of
    France?

Chapter 2: Answers

1. Queen Elizabeth II
2. 1066
3. Winston Churchill
4. RMS Titanic
5. Egyptians
6. Catherine of Aragon
7. 1989
8. Richard III
9. George Washington
10. 1918
11. Christopher Columbus
12. Jamestown
13. 1666
14. Augustus
15. Control of French territory
16. Vladimir Lenin
17. Queen Victoria
18. Sputnik
19. King George V
20. 1912
21. Margaret Thatcher
22. Bucephalus
23. Roman Empire
24. New Amsterdam
25. Hatshepsut
26. Battle of Waterloo
27. Johannes Gutenberg

28.Rifles
29.Hawaii
30.1962
31.Nelson Mandela
32.Magna Carta
33.Abraham Lincoln
34.1903
35.Pompeii
36.Joseph Stalin
37.Latin
38.1989
39.Apollo 11
40.King George III
41.Cleopatra
42.Mayflower
43.Indira Gandhi
44.Robert Falcon Scott
45.1588
46.Ferdinand Magellan
47.1999
48.Mongol Empire
49.World War I
50.Louis XIV

Chapter 3: Geography

1. What is the longest river in the UK?
2. Which country is known as the Land of the Rising Sun?
3. What is the smallest country in the world by area?
4. Which ocean lies on the west coast of the United States?
5. What is the capital city of New Zealand?
6. Which river flows through the city of Paris?
7. What is the deepest lake in the UK?
8. What is the capital of Iceland?
9. In which country would you find the Great Barrier Reef?
10. What is the highest mountain in Africa?
11. Which desert covers much of northern Africa?
12. What is the largest country in South America?
13. Which US state has the nickname "The Sunshine State"?
14. What is the capital city of Canada?
15. How many countries share a border with Germany?
16. Which island country is located southeast of India?
17. What is the largest island in the Mediterranean Sea?

18. Which European city is known for its canals and gondolas?
19. What is the name of the mountain range that separates Europe from Asia?
20. Which UK city is known as the birthplace of The Beatles?
21. What is the largest lake in the UK by surface area?
22. What is the capital city of Portugal?
23. Which country has the most volcanoes?
24. What is the smallest continent by land area?
25. In which ocean is the island of Madagascar located?
26. Which Asian country has the most people?
27. What is the highest peak in the Alps?
28. Which country is famous for its fjords?
29. What is the official language of Egypt?
30. Which UK river is the longest?
31. Which country has the most UNESCO World Heritage Sites?
32. What is the capital city of South Korea?
33. Which city is home to the Colosseum?
34. What is the largest city in Australia by population?
35. What is the southernmost continent on Earth?
36. Which UK city is known for its Roman baths?

37. What is the currency of Mexico?
38. What body of water separates Saudi Arabia from Africa?
39. What is the driest desert in the world?
40. Which country is bordered by both the Atlantic and Indian Oceans?
41. What is the name of the sea located between Greece and Turkey?
42. Which country is home to the world's tallest waterfall, Angel Falls?
43. What is the capital city of Finland?
44. In which country would you find the city of Dubrovnik?
45. What is the largest coral reef system in the world?
46. Which US city is known as the Windy City?
47. What is the capital of the Maldives?
48. Which mountain is known as the "Roof of the World"?
49. Which country is completely surrounded by South Africa?
50. What is the longest railway line in the world?

Chapter 3: Answers

1. River Severn
2. Japan
3. Vatican City
4. Pacific Ocean
5. Wellington
6. River Seine
7. Loch Morar
8. Reykjavik
9. Australia
10. Mount Kilimanjaro
11. Sahara Desert
12. Brazil
13. Florida
14. Ottawa
15. 9
16. Sri Lanka
17. Sicily
18. Venice
19. Ural Mountains
20. Liverpool
21. Loch Lomond
22. Lisbon
23. Indonesia
24. Australia
25. Indian Ocean
26. China
27. Mont Blanc

28. Norway
29. Arabic
30. River Thames
31. Italy
32. Seoul
33. Rome
34. Sydney
35. Antarctica
36. Bath
37. Peso
38. Red Sea
39. Atacama Desert
40. South Africa
41. Aegean Sea
42. Venezuela
43. Helsinki
44. Croatia
45. Great Barrier Reef
46. Chicago
47. Malé
48. Mount Everest
49. Lesotho
50. Trans-Siberian Railway

Chapter 4: Music

1. Which band had a hit with "Wonderwall" in the 1990s?
2. Who is the lead singer of Coldplay?
3. Which female artist released the album *21*?
4. What was the name of The Beatles' first single?
5. Which song by Elton John was rewritten for Princess Diana's funeral?
6. Who won the Eurovision Song Contest for the UK in 2022?
7. What is Adele's surname?
8. Which rapper featured on Ed Sheeran's song "Shape of You" remix?
9. Which British girl group had hits with "Wannabe" and "Say You'll Be There"?
10. What was David Bowie's alter ego in the 1970s?
11. Who was known as the "King of Pop"?
12. Which band was Freddie Mercury the lead singer of?
13. What is the best-selling album of all time?
14. Who had a hit with "Rolling in the Deep"?
15. Which instrument is Yo-Yo Ma famous for playing?
16. Who was the first British solo artist to have a number one hit in the US?

17. What is the title of Queen's 1980 hit that became popular in sports arenas?
18. Which singer was known as the "Queen of Soul"?
19. What is the name of Beyoncé's debut solo album?
20. Who is the drummer for The Rolling Stones?
21. Which classical composer wrote the "Moonlight Sonata"?
22. Who is the best-selling female artist of all time?
23. Which pop group sang "Dancing Queen"?
24. Who had a hit with "Shake It Off" in 2014?
25. What was The Who's rock opera called?
26. Who sang the theme song for the James Bond film *Skyfall*?
27. Which music festival is held annually in Somerset, England?
28. What was Elvis Presley's first UK number one single?
29. Who is known as the "Godfather of Soul"?
30. What instrument does Ed Sheeran primarily play?
31. Which boy band was Harry Styles a member of?
32. Who had a number one hit with "Wuthering Heights" in 1978?
33. Which duo performed the song "Bridge Over Troubled Water"?

34. What was the title of Michael Jackson's first solo album?
35. Who was the lead guitarist for The Beatles?
36. What year did the Live Aid concert take place?
37. Which band is known for the hit "Sweet Child O' Mine"?
38. Who was the first woman inducted into the Rock and Roll Hall of Fame?
39. Which song by Queen was re-released after Freddie Mercury's death?
40. What is Elton John's real name?
41. Which artist is known as the "Piano Man"?
42. Who released the album *Rumours* in 1977?
43. What was Madonna's first UK number one single?
44. Who is the lead singer of U2?
45. What instrument did Louis Armstrong play?
46. Which British band released the album *Dark Side of the Moon*?
47. Who had a hit with "Shape of You"?
48. Which rock band is known for their mascot Eddie the Head?
49. Who sang "Bohemian Rhapsody"?
50. What year did The Spice Girls release "Wannabe"?

Chapter 4: Answers

1. Oasis
2. Chris Martin
3. Adele
4. "Love Me Do"
5. "Candle in the Wind 1997"
6. Sam Ryder
7. Adkins
8. Stormzy
9. Spice Girls
10. Ziggy Stardust
11. Michael Jackson
12. Queen
13. *Thriller*
14. Adele
15. Cello
16. Petula Clark
17. "We Will Rock You"
18. Aretha Franklin
19. *Dangerously in Love*
20. Charlie Watts
21. Ludwig van Beethoven
22. Madonna
23. ABBA
24. Taylor Swift
25. *Tommy*
26. Adele
27. Glastonbury

28."Heartbreak Hotel"
29.James Brown
30.Guitar
31.One Direction
32.Kate Bush
33.Simon & Garfunkel
34.*Off the Wall*
35.George Harrison
36.1985
37.Guns N' Roses
38.Tina Turner
39."These Are the Days of Our Lives"
40.Reginald Dwight
41.Billy Joel
42.Fleetwood Mac
43."Into the Groove"
44.Bono
45.Trumpet
46.Pink Floyd
47.Ed Sheeran
48.Iron Maiden
49.Queen
50.1996

Chapter 5: TV & Film

1. Which actor plays James Bond in *No Time to Die*?
2. What is the longest-running soap opera in the UK?
3. Who directed the movie *Inception*?
4. Which TV series features the character, Sheldon Cooper?
5. What is the name of the pub in *EastEnders*?
6. Who won the Oscar for Best Actor in 2023?
7. Which British TV series is set in the fictional village of Dibley?
8. Who starred as the titular character in *Mary Poppins Returns*?
9. Which animated movie features a character called Woody?
10. What year did *Game of Thrones* first air on television?
11. Who played the character of Harry Potter in the film series?
12. Which actress played Queen Elizabeth II in the first two seasons of *The Crown*?
13. In what year was the first Star Wars movie released?
14. What is the highest-grossing film of all time?
15. Who directed *Schindler's List*?

16. What is the name of the coffee shop in *Friends*?
17. Which actor starred as the Terminator in the 1984 film?
18. What was the name of the ship in the *Pirates of the Caribbean* movies?
19. Who is the host of the UK version of *The Great British Bake Off* (as of 2024)?
20. Which film features the famous line "I'll be back"?
21. What year did the first episode of *Doctor Who* air?
22. Who played the Joker in *The Dark Knight*?
23. Which film won Best Picture at the Oscars in 2024?
24. Which animated series features characters named Homer, Marge, Bart, Lisa, and Maggie?
25. What is the name of the spaceship in *Star Trek*?
26. Who voiced the character of Simba in the 2019 remake of *The Lion King*?
27. Which actress stars in the TV series *Killing Eve*?
28. What is the highest-rated TV show on IMDb?
29. Who played the character of Forrest Gump?
30. What is the title of the final film in the *Harry Potter* series?

31. In which movie does the character Jack Dawson appear?

32. Which UK TV series is set in a hospital called Holby City?

33. Who directed *The Lord of the Rings* trilogy?

34. What is the name of the dragon in *The Hobbit* films?

35. Which actor played Tony Stark in the Marvel Cinematic Universe?

36. What is the fictional setting of *Peaky Blinders*?

37. Who starred as Lara Croft in the 2001 film *Tomb Raider*?

38. Which movie features the song "My Heart Will Go On"?

39. Who played the character of Eleven in *Stranger Things*?

40. What year did *The Simpsons* first air?

41. Which TV show features a character named Don Draper?

42. Who directed the movie *Jurassic Park*?

43. In which film series would you find the character Legolas?

44. What is the name of the school in *Dead Poets Society*?

45. Which actor plays the character of John Wick?

46. What is the highest-grossing animated film of all time?

47. Who starred as the titular character in
     Edward Scissorhands?
48. What is the name of the kingdom in *Frozen*?
49. Which TV show popularised the phrase
     "Winter is Coming"?
50. Who directed *Pulp Fiction*?

Chapter 5: Answers

1. Daniel Craig
2. *Coronation Street*
3. Christopher Nolan
4. *The Big Bang Theory*
5. The Queen Vic
6. Brendan Fraser
7. *The Vicar of Dibley*
8. Emily Blunt
9. *Toy Story*
10. 2011
11. Daniel Radcliffe
12. Claire Foy
13. 1977
14. *Avatar*
15. Steven Spielberg
16. Central Perk
17. Arnold Schwarzenegger
18. The Black Pearl
19. Alison Hammond
20. *The Terminator*
21. 1963
22. Heath Ledger
23. *Everything Everywhere All at Once*
24. *The Simpsons*
25. USS Enterprise
26. Donald Glover
27. Sandra Oh

28.*Breaking Bad*
29.Tom Hanks
30.*Harry Potter and the Deathly Hallows: Part2*
31.*Titanic*
32.*Casualty*
33.Peter Jackson
34.Smaug
35.Robert Downey Jr.
36.Birmingham
37.Angelina Jolie
38.*Titanic*
39.Millie Bobby Brown
40.1989
41.*Mad Men*
42.Steven Spielberg
43.*The Lord of the Rings*
44.Welton Academy
45.Keanu Reeves
46.*Frozen II*
47.Johnny Depp
48.Arendelle
49.*Game of Thrones*
50.Quentin Tarantino

Chapter 6: Sports

1. Which team won the Premier League in the 2022-2023 season?
2. Who holds the record for the most Wimbledon men's singles titles?
3. In which sport would you perform a slam dunk?
4. Who was the England football manager during the 2018 World Cup?
5. How many players are there in a rugby union team?
6. Which country hosted the 2023 Rugby World Cup?
7. Who won the men's singles title at the 2024 Australian Open?
8. Which F1 driver holds the most world championships?
9. What is the nickname of Manchester United's home ground?
10. In cricket, what is a score of 100 called?
11. Who was the first athlete to run a mile in under 4 minutes?
12. Which country has won the most FIFA World Cup titles?
13. Who won the gold medal in men's tennis at the 2024 Olympics?
14. What is the highest possible score in 10-pin bowling?

15. Who is known as "The King of Clay" in tennis?
16. In which sport would you use a shuttlecock?
17. What is the length of an Olympic swimming pool?
18. Who was the captain of England's cricket team during the 2019 World Cup?
19. Which country won the first Rugby World Cup?
20. Who holds the record for the most goals in a single Premier League season?
21. In which year were the first modern Olympic Games held?
22. What is the maximum break in snooker?
23. Which sport is played at Wimbledon?
24. Who was the top scorer in the Premier League 2023-2024 season?
25. What is the name of the trophy awarded at the end of the NFL season?
26. Which boxer was known as "The Greatest"?
27. How many points is a touchdown worth in American football?
28. In which country did the sport of golf originate?
29. Who is the all-time top scorer in the FIFA World Cup?
30. What is the term for three strikes in a row in bowling?

31. Which female gymnast has the most
Olympic medals?
32. Who was the first British driver to win the
Formula 1 World Championship?
33. What is the national sport of Japan?
34. Which city hosted the 2024 Summer
Olympics?
35. In cricket, what does the term "LBW" stand
for?
36. Who is the current UFC heavyweight
champion (as of 2024)?
37. What is the diameter of a basketball hoop?
38. Who holds the record for the fastest 100m
sprint?
39. Which football club is nicknamed "The
Gunners"?
40. How many sets are played in a Grand Slam
tennis match?
41. Which country won the 2023 ICC Cricket
World Cup?
42. What is the distance of a marathon?
43. Who is the captain of the England women's
football team (as of 2024)?
44. In which sport would you find a pommel
horse?
45. Who scored the winning goal in the 1966
FIFA World Cup Final?
46. What is the term for a score of one under
par in golf?

47. Who was the first woman to win a Grand Slam title?
48. What is the weight of an Olympic barbell?
49. Which sport is known as "the beautiful game"?
50. Who holds the record for the most Olympic gold medals?

Chapter 6: Answers

1. Manchester City
2. Roger Federer
3. Basketball
4. Gareth Southgate
5. 15 players
6. France
7. Novak Djokovic
8. Lewis Hamilton
9. Old Trafford
10. A century
11. Roger Bannister
12. Brazil
13. Carlos Alcaraz
14. 300 points
15. Rafael Nadal
16. Badminton
17. 50 meters
18. Eoin Morgan
19. New Zealand
20. Erling Haaland
21. 1896
22. 147
23. Tennis
24. Erling Haaland
25. Vince Lombardi Trophy
26. Muhammad Ali
27. 6 points

28.Scotland
29.Miroslav Klose
30.A turkey
31.Simone Biles
32.Mike Hawthorn
33.Sumo wrestling
34.Paris
35.Leg Before Wicket (LBW)
36.Jon Jones
37.18 inches (45.72 cm)
38.Usain Bolt
39.Arsenal
40.5 sets (men), 3 sets (women)
41.India
42.42.195 kilometres
43.Leah Williamson
44.Gymnastics
45.Geoff Hurst
46.Birdie
47.Maureen Connolly
48.20 kg (men's barbell)
49.Football (soccer)
50.Michael Phelps

Chapter 7: Food & Drink

1. What is the main ingredient of haggis?
2. Which cocktail is made with gin, vermouth, and Campari?
3. What is the traditional accompaniment to fish and chips in the UK?
4. What is the national dish of India?
5. What type of pastry is used for a Cornish pasty?
6. Which soft drink was originally invented as a medicine?
7. What is the most popular takeaway food in the UK?
8. In which year was Coca-Cola first sold?
9. What is a Yorkshire pudding traditionally served with?
10. What type of cheese is used in a traditional Greek salad?
11. Which fruit is known as the "king of fruits"?
12. What is the main ingredient in guacamole?
13. Which spice is made from dried and ground ginger root?
14. What type of alcohol is used in a traditional mojito?
15. What is the Italian term for "starter" or "appetiser"?
16. What is the national drink of Scotland?

17. Which popular drink is made from fermented apples?
18. What is tofu made from?
19. In which country did the dish sushi originate?
20. What is the main ingredient in a traditional ratatouille?
21. Which country is the largest producer of olive oil?
22. What type of food is a pumpernickel?
23. What is the name of the flatbread often served with Indian curry?
24. Which dessert is known as the "Queen of Puddings"?
25. What is the primary ingredient of a Bloody Mary cocktail?
26. What type of milk is traditionally used to make mozzarella cheese?
27. What fruit is used to make a Black Forest gâteau?
28. Which country is known for its dish paella?
29. What is the main ingredient in a Margherita pizza?
30. What is the most expensive spice in the world by weight?
31. What is the French term for a three-course meal?
32. What type of pastry is used in a traditional French éclair?

33. What is the name of the beer commonly served at Oktoberfest?
34. Which type of fish is used in a traditional British kedgeree?
35. What is the main ingredient in a falafel?
36. Which country is famous for its wine region called Bordeaux?
37. What is the name of the Japanese dish that features skewered grilled chicken?
38. What is the name of the traditional Irish stew?
39. Which fruit has varieties called Granny Smith and Pink Lady?
40. What is the national dish of Mexico?
41. What ingredient gives gin its distinctive flavour?
42. Which dessert is made from whipped egg whites and sugar?
43. Which sauce is traditionally served with roast beef?
44. What is the main ingredient of a Welsh rareblt?
45. In which city would you find the famous market known for its cheesesteaks?
46. What type of nuts are used to make marzipan?
47. Which country is the largest exporter of coffee?

48. What is the name of the French dessert made from layers of puff pastry and cream?
49. Which vegetable is traditionally used in colcannon?
50. What type of bread is used to make a Reuben sandwich?

Chapter 7: Answers

1. Sheep's pluck (liver, heart, and lungs)
2. Negroni
3. Mushy peas
4. Curry
5. Shortcrust pastry
6. Coca-Cola
7. Chinese food
8. 1886
9. Roast beef and gravy
10. Feta cheese
11. Durian
12. Avocado
13. Ginger
14. Rum
15. Antipasto
16. Whisky
17. Cider
18. Soybeans
19. Japan
20. Eggplant (aubergine), zucchini, and tomato
21. Spain
22. Rye bread
23. Naan
24. Queen of Puddings
25. Tomato juice
26. Buffalo milk
27. Cherries

28. Spain
29. Tomatoes, mozzarella, and basil
30. Saffron
31. Menu du jour
32. Choux pastry
33. Märzen
34. Smoked haddock
35. Chickpeas
36. France
37. Yakitori
38. Irish stew
39. Apples
40. Tacos
41. Juniper berries
42. Meringue
43. Horseradish sauce
44. Cheese
45. Philadelphia
46. Almonds
47. Brazil
48. Mille-feuille
49. Kale
50. Rye bread

Chapter 8: Science & Nature

1. What is the chemical formula for water?
2. Which planet is known as the Red Planet?
3. What is the hardest natural substance on Earth?
4. How many hearts does an octopus have?
5. What is the study of fungi called?
6. What gas do plants absorb from the atmosphere?
7. Who developed the theory of relativity?
8. How many bones are there in the human body?
9. What is the largest mammal in the world?
10. What is the process by which plants make their food called?
11. What is the main gas found in the Earth's atmosphere?
12. What is the powerhouse of the cell?
13. Which element is represented by the symbol 'O'?
14. What is the most common blood type in humans?
15. Which planet has the most moons?
16. What is the term for animals that only eat plants?
17. Which type of rock is formed from cooled lava?
18. Who was the first person to orbit the Earth?

19. What is the chemical symbol for sodium?
20. What is the fastest land animal?
21. Which organ in the human body is primarily responsible for filtering blood?
22. What is the smallest particle of an element?
23. Which planet is closest to the Sun?
24. What is the name of the largest ocean on Earth?
25. How many chromosomes are in a human cell?
26. Which mammal is known for laying eggs?
27. What type of tree produces acorns?
28. What is the name of the galaxy that contains our Solar System?
29. What is the most abundant element in the universe?
30. What is the term for a scientist who studies weather?
31. How many legs does a spider have?
32. Which bird has the largest wingspan?
33. What is the boiling point of water in Celsius?
34. What part of the plant conducts photosynthesis?
35. What is the largest internal organ in the human body?
36. What is a group of lions called?
37. Which planet has rings made of ice and rock?

38. What is the name of the device used to measure air pressure?

39. Which vitamin is produced when the human body is exposed to sunlight?

40. What type of celestial object is a supernova?

41. What is the deepest part of the world's oceans?

42. Which dinosaur's name means "swift seizer"?

43. What is the largest flower in the world?

44. Which gas is commonly used in balloons to make them float?

45. What is the smallest species of bird?

46. Which process turns liquid water into vapor?

47. How many planets are there in our Solar System?

48. What is the most venomous snake in the world?

49. What type of animal is a Komodo dragon?

50. Who was the first woman to win a Nobel Prize?

Chapter 8: Answers

1. H_2O
2. Mars
3. Diamond
4. Three
5. Mycology
6. Carbon dioxide
7. Albert Einstein
8. 206
9. Blue whale
10. Photosynthesis
11. Nitrogen
12. Mitochondria
13. Oxygen (O)
14. O positive
15. Jupiter
16. Herbivore
17. Igneous rock
18. Yuri Gagarin
19. Na
20. Cheetah
21. Kidneys
22. Atom
23. Mercury
24. Pacific Ocean
25. 46
26. Platypus
27. Oak

28. Milky Way
29. Hydrogen
30. Meteorologist
31. Eight
32. Albatross
33. 100°C
34. Leaf
35. Liver
36. Pride
37. Saturn
38. Barometer
39. Vitamin D
40. Exploding star
41. Mariana Trench
42. Velociraptor
43. Rafflesia
44. Helium
45. Hummingbird
46. Evaporation
47. Eight
48. Inland Taipan
49. Reptile
50. Marie Curie

Chapter 9: 2023 Recap

1. What was the name of Prince Harry's memoir published in January?
2. At the beginning of the year which country re-opened its borders to international visitors three years after the beginning of the covid pandemic?
3. What did Kylie Jenner wear to the Schiaparelli fashion show in January?
4. What is the name of the fungal infection that caused a global pandemic in the TV series The Last of Us?
5. After winning four Grammys in February, Beyoncé is now the most awarded artist in the prize's history, but how many Grammys in total does she have?
6. During the BAFTAs in February, what was the meme that went viral?
7. What did Rihanna reveal during her Super Bowl halftime show?
8. Who won the Best Actress award at the Oscars?
9. The Scandoval cheating scandal shocked the reality TV world in March, who was accused of having the sixth month long affair?
10. Why was Gary Lineker forced off his hosting duties for Match of the Day in March?

11. What date did Taylor Swift's Eras Tour commence?

12. In April which country became the 31st country to join NATO?

13. Netflix's Beef was one of the most popular shows of the year, who were the two lead actors in the series?

14. Who won the Women's Six Nations?

15. What was the codename for King Charles coronation?

16. Where was King Charles' coronation held?

17. And which guest couldn't find her seat at the coronation?

18. Who was the actor who took on the role of Ariel in the live action Disney movie The Little Mermaid?

19. What was the name of Kylie Minogue's viral single released in May?

20. How many months did the WGA strike go on for?

21. What city hosted the Eurovision contest this year?

22. Who won the men's 2022 – 2023 Premier League?

23. Who's set was famously cut short at Glastonbury?

24. What is the name of the Barbie played by Kate McKinnon in the Barbie movie?

25. In the Barbie film what is Ken's job?

26. Who ended Novak Djokovic's winning streak at Wimbledon?
27. Which Greek Island suffered serious wild fires which caused many tourists to flee it?
28. What was the final score of the FIFA Women's World Cup final match between England and Spain?
29. What is the name of the social media app designed by Meta, aimed to rival Twitter/X?
30. How was a Just Stop Oil protestor removed from an Ashes test match at Lords?
31. In August which former US president's mugshot went viral?
32. What is the name of the TikTok trend that sees people showcase their meals of mismatched items?
33. Which actor was Kylie Jenner revealed to be dating?
34. Which fashion designer stepped down from Alexander McQueen after 26 years at the brand?
35. In September what epidemic was said to be being brought over to the UK from Paris?
36. Who won the women's singles title at the US Open?
37. NASA declared this summer the hottest on record, but what was the average global temperature that summer? (closest answer wins)

38. Who was the only non-Red Bull F1 driver to win a Grand Prix race in the 2023 Formula One World Championship?
39. Who narrated Britney Spears' highly anticipated memoir The Woman in Me for the audio book version?
40. What product did Kim Kardashian launch for her brand Skims that caused some backlash?
41. Who won Big Brother 2023?
42. What is the real name of the TikToker who went viral as 'Tube Girl'?
43. What car did Victoria Beckham's dad used to drop her off in at school as revealed by the Beckham documentary?
44. Which Love Island contestant appeared in three versions of the show this year?
45. Which former British Prime Minister was appointed Foreign Secretary in November?
46. What milestone birthday did Prince Charles reach this year?
47. Which music artist shaved his hair off in November, causing the internet to lose its mind?
48. What was the Oxford English Dictionary word of the year?

49. As of December 2023, how many users does Chat GPT now have (closest answer wins)?
50. Which politician starred on I'm a Celebrity Get Me Out of Here?

Chapter 9: Answers

1. Spare
2. China
3. A dress with a lion's head on it
4. Cordyceps
5. 32
6. Ariana DeBose rapping 'Angela Bassett did the thing'
7. That she was pregnant with her second child
8. Michelle Yeoh
9. Tom Sandoval and Raquel Leviss
10. He was a in a impartiality row with the BBC over his Twitter after he criticised the language used in a government asylum policy
11. 17th March 2023
12. Finland
13. Steven Yeun and Ali Wong
14. England
15. Operation Golden Orb
16. Westminster Abbcy
17. Katy Perry
18. Halle Bailey
19. 'Padam Padam'
20. 4 months from 2 May 2023 – 27 Sept 2023
21. Liverpool, UK
22. Manchester City

23. Lana Del Rey
24. Weird Barbie
25. Beach
26. Carlos Alcaraz
27. Rhodes
28. Spain won 1-0 to England
29. Threads
30. England wicket-keeper Jonny Bairstow picked up one of the protestors and moved him off the pitch
31. Donald Trump
32. Girl Dinner
33. Timothée Chalamet
34. Sarah Burton
35. A bed bug invasion
36. Coco Gauff
37. 16.77C
38. Carlos Sainz at Ferrari
39. Michelle Williams
40. A bra with nipples on it
41. Jordan Sangha
42. Sabrina Bahsoon
43. A Rolls Royce
44. Scott van-der-Sluis on Love Island UK, Love Island US, and Love Island Games
45. David Cameron
46. His 75th birthday on 14th November 2023
47. Harry Styles
48. Rizz

49.Around 180.5million
50.Nigel Farage

Chapter 10: 2024 Recap

1. Which radio show celebrated its 100th anniversary on 1st January 2024?
2. The release of which TV show prompted then Prime Minister Rishi Sunak to say he would overturn and compensate hundreds of postmasters?
3. Which English singer finally became an EGOT after winning an Emmy?
4. In February, an unlicensed Willy Wonka experience went viral, but where did it take place?
5. Which celebrity launched the beauty brand Cécred in February?
6. Which music company pulled all of their artists' songs from TikTok?
7. Who performed at the Super Bowl Half Time show?
8. Raye made history at the BRIT awards by winning a record number of wins, so how many awards did she win?
9. The shirt worn by Colin Firth in BBC's Pride and Prejudice was sold at a charity auction, how much did it go for?
10. Meghan, The Duchess of Sussex soft-launched a lifestyle brand in March, what was it called?

11. Which country became the 32nd to join NATO?

12. In March, which iconic British confectionary brand celebrated its 200th anniversary?

13. Beyoncé released her eighth studio album this year, what is its name?

14. What was the name of the single Sabrina Carpenter released in April?

15. New York was struck with one of its worst earthquakes in over 100 years in April. What was the magnitude?

16. What sport was the movie Challengers based on?

17. In April, Russ Cook, aka the Hardest Geezer, made the news, but was for?

18. On TikTok a baby went viral for wanting to go to a hotel. Which hotel was it?

19. What was the name of the song that won Eurovision?

20. In May what natural phenomenon, previously unable to be seen from the UK, was visible?

21. Which singer allegedly said "This is going to ruin the tour" after being arrested in June?

22. Which fashion designer showed his final collection in June before retiring?

23. A film came out in June which was the first to overtake Barbie in the Box Office, making $1.46 billion worldwide. What film was it?

24. Which country won the Euros in July?

25. Taylor Swift toured the Eras Tour in the UK, for every support act she had in the UK that you can name, you get a point.

26. Who won the men's singles at Wimbledon?

27. In July Keir Starmer became Prime Minister, but when was the last time we had a Labour Prime Minister prior to this?

28. According to Charli XCX, what kind of summer did we all have?

29. Which country won the Olympics?

30. What date was the UK's hottest day of the year, which was recorded at 34.8C, was it a) July 27th B) 5th August or C)12th August?

31. Jason and Travis Kelce signed a new podcast deal with Amazon in August. How much was the deal worth?

32. Which country banned X (formerly known as Twitter) in August?

33. Which common vegetable went viral over summer after a TikTok creator said, "sometimes you just need to eat an entire X" and proceeded to show fans the best way to prepare it?

34. Which Premier League football club did Enzo Maresca join in summer?

35. What is the name of the baby pygmy hippo that went viral earlier this year?

36. What was the job of Kamala Harris' running mate Tim Walz before going into politics?
37. Which British royal princess announced her second pregnancy in October?
38. What was the name of the super full moon that occurred in October?
39. What launch did Elon Musk reveal?
40. What did the Oxford University Press declare their word/phrase of the year?
41. Which celebrity turned up to their own viral look-a-like competition in New York?
42. What are the names of the book and author who won this year's Booker prize?
43. What is the runtime for Wicked Part 1 which premiered in cinemas on 22nd November?
44. Max Verstappen won his fourth F1 world championship during the Las Vegas GP, but he didn't win the race, who did?
45. Who won The Great British Bake Off on 26th November?

Chapter 10: Answers

1. Shipping Forecast
2. Mr Bates vs The Post Office
3. Elton John
4. Glasgow, Scotland
5. Beyoncé
6. Universal Music Group
7. Usher
8. Six
9. £25,000
10. American Riviera Orchard
11. Sweden
12. Cadbury
13. Cowboy Carter
14. 'Espresso'
15. 4.8
16. Tennis
17. He became the first person to run the length of Africa
18. The Four Seasons Orlando
19. 'The Code'
20. The Northern Lights
21. Justin Timberlake
22. Dries Van Noten
23. Inside Out 2
24. Spain

25. Paramore, Suki Waterhouse, Maisie Peters,
Raye, Griff, Sofia Isella, and Holly
Humberstone
26. Carlos Alcaraz
27. Gordon Brown served as Prime Minister
from 2007 to 2010
28. A BRAT summer
29. The United States
30. 12th August
31. $100million
32. Brazil
33. Cucumber
34. Chelsea
35. Moo Deng
36. He was a geography teacher
37. Princess Beatrice
38. Hunter Supermoon
39. Humanoid Robots
40. Brain rot
41. Timothée Chalamet
42. Orbital by Samantha Harvey
43. 2 hours and 41 minutes
44. George Russell
45. Georgie Grasso

Chapter 11: Politics

1. Who was the UK Prime Minister during the Brexit referendum in 2016?
2. What is the name of the official residence of the UK Prime Minister?
3. Which party did Tony Blair represent when he became Prime Minister in 1997?
4. In which year did the Good Friday Agreement bring peace to Northern Ireland?
5. Who succeeded David Cameron as UK Prime Minister?
6. What is the upper house of the UK Parliament called?
7. Which political leader became the first female Chancellor of Germany?
8. What year did the Scottish Independence Referendum take place?
9. Who was the leader of the UK Labour Party before Keir Starmer?
10. Which country did the UK vote to leave in the Brexit referendum?
11. Who was the first female Prime Minister of the United Kingdom?
12. What is the name of the document that outlines the laws and principles of the US government?

13. Who was the first President of the United States?

14. In which year did Margaret Thatcher become Prime Minister of the UK?

15. Which political party is traditionally associated with the colour red in the UK?

16. Who was the longest-serving British Prime Minister of the 20th century?

17. What is the name of the building where the US Congress meets?

18. Who was the Prime Minister of the UK during World War II?

19. What is the name of the legislative body of the European Union?

20. Who was the first Black President of South Africa?

21. What year did the Berlin Wall fall, symbolising the end of the Cold War?

22. Which US President was involved in the Watergate scandal?

23. Who was the first female Speaker of the House of Commons in the UK?

24. In which country did the Arab Spring protests begin in 2010?

25. Which UK political leader was known as "The Iron Lady"?

26. Who is the current monarch of the United Kingdom (as of 2024)?

27. Which UK political party is traditionally associated with environmental issues?
28. What is the official name of the political system in North Korea?
29. Who was the UK Prime Minister during the Iraq War in 2003?
30. In which year did the UK join the European Economic Community (EEC)?
31. Who was the first President of Russia after the fall of the Soviet Union?
32. Which political figure is known for delivering the "I Have a Dream" speech?
33. Who became the youngest Prime Minister of the UK in the 21st century?
34. What is the title of the head of government in Canada?
35. Who led the Indian independence movement against British rule?
36. Which political party won the most seats in the 2019 UK General Election?
37. What is the term for a political system where a single party controls the government?
38. Who was the leader of the Soviet Union during the Cuban Missile Crisis?
39. What is the role of the Chancellor of the Exchequer in the UK government?
40. In which year did Nelson Mandela become President of South Africa?

41. What is the term used for the right to vote
    in political elections?
42. Who was the first woman to be elected as
    President of a country?
43. Which UK political leader delivered the
    "People's Vote" campaign for a second
    Brexit referendum?
44. What is the title of the leader of the House
    of Lords in the UK?
45. Who was the US President during the
    signing of the Paris Climate Agreement?
46. What is the maximum length of time
    between general elections in the UK?
47. Who was the founder of the Chinese
    Communist Party and led the country from
    1949 to 1976?
48. Which Prime Minister is credited with the
    introduction of the National Health Service
    (NHS) in the UK?
49. What is the main legislative body of Japan
    called?
50. Who succeeded Angela Merkel as
    Chancellor of Germany?

Chapter 11: Answers

1. David Cameron
2. 10 Downing Street
3. Labour
4. 1998
5. Theresa May
6. House of Lords
7. Angela Merkel
8. 2014
9. Jeremy Corbyn
10. European Union
11. Margaret Thatcher
12. The Constitution
13. George Washington
14. 1979
15. Labour Party
16. Margaret Thatcher
17. Capitol Hill
18. Winston Churchill
19. European Parliament
20. Nelson Mandela
21. 1989
22. Richard Nixon
23. Betty Boothroyd
24. Tunisia
25. Margaret Thatcher
26. King Charles III
27. Green Party

28. Single-party state
29. Tony Blair
30. 1973
31. Boris Yeltsin
32. Martin Luther King Jr.
33. Rishi Sunak
34. Prime Minister
35. Mahatma Gandhi
36. Conservative Party
37. Totalitarianism
38. Nikita Khrushchev
39. Oversees economic and financial matters
40. 1994
41. Suffrage
42. Vigdís Finnbogadóttir
43. Jo Swinson
44. Lord Speaker
45. Barack Obama
46. 5 years
47. Mao Zedong
48. Clement Attlee
49. National Diet
50. Olaf Scholz

Chapter 12: The 2000's Decade

1. In what year did Michael Jackson die?
2. What was the UK's best-selling book of the 2000s?
3. Prince Charles married Camilla Parker Bowles during which month in 2005?
4. What was the highest grossing movie of the decade?
5. Who became British Prime Minister in 2007?
6. England celebrated victory in the 2003 Rugby World Cup, thanks to a winning drop goal from which player?
7. 'Friends' finished in 2004 after how many seasons?
8. Which celebrity shaved her head during a now-infamous breakdown in 2007?
9. In which American state did the 2002 Winter Olympics take place?
10. Popstars launched in 2001, heralding a new era of music acts finding fame through TV talent shows. Which group won the first series?
11. What was Limewire?
12. For which disease did the World Health Organisation issue a global alert in 2003?
13. Young socialites Paris Hilton and Nicole Richie starred on a 2000s reality show called...

14. Beyoncé's Single Ladies famously lost the accolade for Best Female Videos at the 2009 VMAs. Who won and why was the moment marred by controversy?

15. In March 2002, Halle Berry made history by becoming the first black woman to win an Oscar for Best Actress - for which film?

16. Which was the last Pixar animated film released in the decade?

17. Rihanna received her first number one single with which song in the 00s?

18. Which two famous paintings by Edvard Munch were stolen in 2004 at gunpoint from a museum in Norway?

19. Which family made their EastEnders debut in September 2000?

20. Where did the Russian submarine Kursk sink in 2000?

21. People were shocked when Madonna kissed which star at the 2003 MTV VMAs?

22. What was DW Reed's full name on 'Arthur'?

23. Which future social media giant was launched in 2004?

24. Raven Baxter was a psychic high school student on the Disney Channel. What city did she live in?

25. Which Britain's Got Talent winner had the best-selling album of 2009?

26. What film won the Oscar for Best Picture for 2000?

27. Which series from the 2000s featured the characters Sheldon and Leonard?

28. What is the name of the school Blair and Serena attend at the start of 'Gossip Girl'?

29. Barack Obama became the first African-American to be elected as President in the US during 2008. But who did he beat to the White House in the 2008 US Presidential Election?

30. What were the names of the godparents in "The Fairly OddParents"?

31. Which country's football team won Euro 2008?

32. Who was the winner of the first Big Brother series in the UK in 2000?

33. What channel did Two Pints of Lager and a Packet of Crisps first air on?

34. Which iconic gadget was first released on November 10, 2001?

35. The Charles Ingram 'Who Wants To Be a Millionaire' cheating scandal happened in September of what year?

36. Finish the "Friends" theme song lyric: "Your job's a joke, you're broke, your love life's ___ "

37. After dominating the 90s with their chart-topping R'n'B, Destiny's Child members went solo in the noughties. Who had a UK No.1 hit first?

38. Who became the first woman poet laureate in May 2009?

39. Ready Steady Cook is making a comeback with Radio 2's very own Rylan at the helm. Who hosted the show throughout the noughties, from 2000 to 2010?

40. Apple released its first iPhone smartphone in which year?

41. Coldplay had four Number 1 albums across the decade, starting with 2000 debut 'Parachutes'. They only had one Number 1 single in the 00s, however. What was it?

42. The first ever series of ITV's I'm a Celebrity… Get Me Out of Here! aired in 2002. Who won the very first edition?

43. In 2005, Doctor Who returned to British TV screens for its first full series since 1989 with Christopher Eccleston in the lead role, alongside which singer-turned-actress?

44. The UK's biggest selling single of the 2000s was by a reality show winner. But what was it?

45. Supernanny was a Channel 4 reality show that ran from 2004 to 2008. But what was the name of the eponymous nanny who imparted childcare advice to members of the public?

46. In 2002, which rock and roll family invited cameras into their home for a reality show on MTV?

47. In 2009, the British high street lost which well-known brand, with its final branch closing in January of that year?
48. The term 'podcast' was first coined in which year?
49. The most-viewed series of Britain's Got Talent aired in 2009, with Susan Boyle coming second in the grand final. Who won?
50. She would go on to be one of the best-selling acts of the following decade, but Adele's first album was released in 2008 - what was it called?

Chapter 12: Answers

1. 2009
2. The Da Vinci Code
3. April
4. Avatar
5. Gordon Brown
6. Jonny Wilkinson
7. 10
8. Britney Spears
9. Utah
10. Hearsay
11. An illegal music download application
12. SARS
13. The Simple Life
14. Taylor Swift, who was interrupted by Kanye West saying "Beyoncé had the best video of all time"
15. Monster's Ball
16. Up
17. SOS
18. The Scream and Madonna
19. The Slaters
20. Barents Sea
21. Britney Spears
22. Dora Winifred Read
23. Facebook
24. San Fransisco, California

25. Susan Boyle
26. Gladiator
27. The Big Bang Theory
28. Constance Billard School for Girls
29. John McCain
30. Cosmo and Wanda
31. Spain
32. Craig Phillips
33. BBC
34. iPod
35. 2001
36. D.O.A
37. Kelly Rowland
38. Carol Ann Duffy
39. Ainsley Harriot
40. 2007
41. Viva la Vida
42. Tony Blackburn
43. Billie Piper
44. Will Young - Evergreen
45. Jo Frost
46. The Osbournes
47. Woolworths
48. 2004
49. Diversity
50. 19

Chapter 13: Literature

1. Who wrote *To Kill a Mockingbird*?
2. What is the first book of the *Harry Potter* series?
3. Who created the character Sherlock Holmes?
4. What is the title of the third book in *The Lord of the Rings* series?
5. Which author wrote *1984* and *Animal Farm*?
6. Who is the author of *The Great Gatsby*?
7. What is the longest play written by William Shakespeare?
8. Who wrote the novel *Frankenstein*?
9. In which century was Geoffrey Chaucer's *The Canterbury Tales* written?
10. Who is the author of *Pride and Prejudice*?
11. What was the pen name of Samuel Clemens?
12. Which book begins with the line "Call me Ishmael"?
13. Who wrote the children's book *Matilda*?
14. What genre of literature is *The Odyssey* classified as?
15. Who wrote *The Hitchhiker's Guide to the Galaxy*?
16. What is the title of the first novel in *A Song of Ice and Fire* series?

17. Who wrote *The Catcher in the Rye*?

18. Which novel features the characters Frodo Baggins and Samwise Gamgee?

19. Who is the detective in *Murder on the Orient Express*?

20. What year was *The Hobbit* first published?

21. Who wrote *Jane Eyre*?

22. What was the last book of the Bible to be written?

23. Who wrote *The Picture of Dorian Gray*?

24. Which Russian author wrote *War and Peace*?

25. What is the name of the wizard in J.R.R. Tolkien's books?

26. Who wrote the *His Dark Materials* series?

27. What is the title of the first book in the *Twilight* series?

28. Who wrote *Wuthering Heights*?

29. Who is the main character in *The Old Man and the Sea*?

30. Who wrote the play *Hamlet*?

31. In which city is *The Great Gatsby* set?

32. Which novel is considered the first science fiction book?

33. Who wrote *Dracula*?

34. Which book features the character of Atticus Finch?

35. Who wrote the dystopian novel *Fahrenheit 451*?

36. Who is the author of *The Chronicles of Narnia*?
37. Which poet wrote "The Road Not Taken"?
38. Who is the main antagonist in *The Count of Monte Cristo*?
39. What is the name of the pig leader in *Animal Farm*?
40. Who wrote *The Tale of Peter Rabbit*?
41. What was the title of J.K. Rowling's first published book?
42. Who wrote *Brave New World*?
43. What is the pen name of the author who wrote *The Girl with the Dragon Tattoo*?
44. Which novel features a character named Pip?
45. Who is the author of *The Alchemist*?
46. Who wrote *A Tale of Two Cities*?
47. What is the title of the first book in the *Divergent* series?
48. Who wrote *The Handmaid's Tale*?
49. Which author is known for the detective series featuring Hercule Poirot?
50. Who wrote *The Grapes of Wrath*?

Chapter 13: Answers

1. Harper Lee
2. *Harry Potter and the Philosopher's Stone*
3. Arthur Conan Doyle
4. *The Return of the King*
5. George Orwell
6. F. Scott Fitzgerald
7. *Hamlet*
8. Mary Shelley
9. 14th century
10. Jane Austen
11. Mark Twain
12. *Moby-Dick*
13. Roald Dahl
14. Epic poetry
15. Douglas Adams
16. *A Game of Thrones*
17. J.D. Salinger
18. *The Lord of the Rings*
19. Hercule Poirot
20. 1937
21. Charlotte Brontë
22. Revelation
23. Oscar Wilde
24. Leo Tolstoy
25. Gandalf
26. Philip Pullman
27. *Twilight*

28. Emily Brontë
29. Santiago
30. William Shakespeare
31. New York City
32. *Frankenstein* by Mary Shelley
33. Bram Stoker
34. *To Kill a Mockingbird*
35. Ray Bradbury
36. C.S. Lewis
37. Robert Frost
38. Danglars
39. Napoleon
40. Beatrix Potter
41. *Harry Potter and the Philosopher's Stone*
42. Aldous Huxley
43. Stieg Larsson
44. *Great Expectations* by Charles Dickens
45. Paulo Coelho
46. Charles Dickens
47. *Divergent*
48. Margaret Atwood
49. Agatha Christie
50. John Steinbeck

Chapter 14: Mythology & Folklore

1. Who is the king of the gods in Greek mythology?
2. What is the Norse mythological name for the end of the world?
3. In Egyptian mythology, who is the god of the afterlife?
4. Which Greek hero was known for his 12 labours?
5. What is the name of the hammer wielded by Thor in Norse mythology?
6. Who is the Roman equivalent of the Greek goddess Aphrodite?
7. Who was the first human woman created by the Greek gods?
8. What creature has the body of a lion and the head of a man in Egyptian mythology?
9. Who was the wife of Zeus in Greek mythology?
10. What was the name of King Arthur's magical sword?
11. Who is the god of the underworld in Greek mythology?
12. What is the name of the legendary one-eyed giants in Greek mythology?
13. Who is the Norse god of mischief?
14. Who sailed with the Argonauts in Greek mythology?

15. Who is the Celtic goddess of war and fertility?

16. What creature is said to guard treasure in European folklore?

17. Who was the Greek god of wine?

18. What is the home of the Greek gods called?

19. What mythical bird is reborn from its own ashes?

20. Who was the chief god of the Aztecs?

21. In which mythological city would you find the Minotaur?

22. Who was the Greek goddess of wisdom?

23. What is the name of the Norse tree that connects the nine worlds?

24. Who was the hero that killed the Hydra?

25. Who is the Hindu god of destruction?

26. What is the name of the Irish folklore fairy known for making shoes?

27. Which Egyptian goddess was known for her protective nature and magic?

28. Who was the Greek goddess of the hunt?

29. What was the name of the Greek hero who fought in the Trojan War?

30. Who was the Greek god of the sea?

31. Which figure in Greek mythology was cursed to turn everything he touched into gold?

32. Who is the king of the underworld in Roman mythology?

33. What is the name of the Japanese sun goddess?

34. Who is the father of Zeus in Greek mythology?

35. What is the name of the mythical Norse hall where warriors go after death?

36. Who was the legendary founder of Rome?

37. What was the name of the winged horse in Greek mythology?

38. Who is the trickster figure in many Native American mythologies?

39. What is the Norse god Loki known for?

40. What was the name of the Greek monster with snakes for hair?

41. Who was the Roman god of war?

42. Who is the Celtic god of the sea?

43. What creature is half woman, half fish in folklore?

44. Who was the Norse god of thunder?

45. What is the name of the Greek god of the sun?

46. Which Greek hero's weakness was his heel?

47. Who is the queen of the Greek gods?

48. What mythical creature breathes fire and is found in many cultures' folklore?

49. Who was the god of love in Roman mythology?

50. What is the name of the Greek underworld?

Chapter 14: Answers

1. Zeus
2. Ragnarök
3. Osiris
4. Heracles (Hercules)
5. Mjölnir
6. Venus
7. Pandora
8. Sphinx
9. Hera
10. Excalibur
11. Hades
12. Cyclops
13. Loki
14. Jason
15. Morrigan
16. Dragon
17. Dionysus
18. Mount Olympus
19. Phoenix
20. Huitzilopochtli
21. Labyrinth (Crete)
22. Athena
23. Yggdrasil
24. Heracles
25. Shiva
26. Leprechaun
27. Isis

28. Artemis
29. Achilles
30. Poseidon
31. King Midas
32. Pluto
33. Amaterasu
34. Cronus
35. Valhalla
36. Romulus
37. Pegasus
38. Coyote
39. Mischief and trickery
40. Medusa
41. Mars
42. Manannán mac Lir
43. Mermaid
44. Thor
45. Helios
46. Achilles
47. Hera
48. Dragon
49. Cupid
50. Hades

Chapter 15: Technology

1. Who is known as the father of the internet?
2. What year was the first iPhone released?
3. What does the acronym "Wi-Fi" stand for?
4. Who founded Microsoft with Bill Gates?
5. What was the first video game ever created?
6. What is the name of the AI assistant in Amazon's Echo devices?
7. What does USB stand for?
8. Which social media platform was launched first: Facebook or Twitter?
9. What is the name of the company that created the Android operating system?
10. Who invented the World Wide Web?
11. What was the first commercially successful home video game console?
12. What does the "G" in 5G stand for?
13. Who is credited with inventing the light bulb?
14. What does HTML stand for?
15. Which company created the first graphical web browser?
16. What is the most popular programming language in the world (as of 2024)?
17. Which search engine was founded by Larry Page and Sergey Brin?
18. What year was YouTube founded?

19. What was the name of the first satellite launched into space?
20. Who invented the first computer mouse?
21. What does VPN stand for?
22. Which company developed the Windows operating system?
23. What year was the first email sent?
24. What does RAM stand for in computer terminology?
25. Who is the founder of Tesla, Inc.?
26. What was the name of the first digital camera?
27. What company introduced the floppy disk?
28. What is the term for a network of connected devices that can exchange data?
29. What is Bitcoin?
30. What is the name of Apple's digital assistant?
31. Which tech company's slogan is "Don't be evil"?
32. What is the term for software that is free to use and modify?
33. Which company made the first smartphone?
34. What does AI stand for?
35. What is the name of the humanoid robot created by Hanson Robotics?
36. What year was the first text message sent?

37. Who developed the programming language Python?
38. What does "IoT" stand for?
39. What is the name of the AI language model developed by OpenAI?
40. What is a blockchain?
41. What was the name of the first website ever created?
42. Which company was the first to reach a market value of $1 trillion?
43. What is the name of the AI software that defeated a world champion in the game of Go?
44. What does DNS stand for?
45. What is the maximum capacity of a standard Blu-ray disc?
46. What was the first mass-produced electric car?
47. Which company created the microprocessor?
48. What is the term for malicious software designed to damage or disrupt systems?
49. What is the most widely used web browser (as of 2024)?
50. What does the "C" in CPU stand for?

Chapter 15: Answers

1. Vint Cerf
2. 2007
3. Wireless Fidelity (Note: It is often mistakenly thought to stand for this, but it is a brand name without a true meaning)
4. Paul Allen
5. *Pong*
6. Alexa
7. Universal Serial Bus
8. Facebook (2004), Twitter (2006)
9. Android Inc.
10. Tim Berners-Lee
11. Atari 2600
12. Generation
13. Thomas Edison
14. Hypertext Markup Language
15. Netscape
16. Python
17. Google
18. 2005
19. Sputnik
20. Douglas Engelbart
21. Virtual Private Network
22. Microsoft
23. 1971
24. Random Access Memory
25. Elon Musk

26.Kodak DCS
27.IBM
28.Internet of Things (IoT)
29.Cryptocurrency
30.Siri
31.Google
32.Open-source software
33.IBM Simon
34.Artificial Intelligence
35.Sophia
36.1992
37.Guido van Rossum
38.Internet of Things
39.ChatGPT
40.Decentralised digital ledger
41.info.cern.ch
42.Apple
43.AlphaGo
44.Domain Name System
45.25 GB (single layer)
46.Tesla Roadster
47.Intel
48.Malware
49.Google Chrome
50.Central

Chapter 16: Art & Design

1. Who painted the *Mona Lisa*?
2. What is the art style characterised by distorted figures and surreal landscapes?
3. Who designed the Eiffel Tower?
4. What is the name of the technique used in painting where small dots of colour are applied?
5. Who painted the ceiling of the Sistine Chapel?
6. Which artist is famous for his melting clocks in the painting *The Persistence of Memory*?
7. What is the most expensive painting ever sold?
8. Who created the sculpture, *David*?
9. What art movement is Vincent van Gogh associated with?
10. What material is traditionally used in the Japanese art of origami?
11. What is the primary medium used by sculptors?
12. Who is known as the father of modern architecture?
13. What is the term for the art of beautiful handwriting?
14. What is the most common type of paint used by artists today?

15. What is the process of designing buildings called?
16. Who painted *The Starry Night*?
17. What is the name of the ancient art of Japanese flower arranging?
18. What is the technique called where an artist carves into wood to create a print?
19. Who was the artist behind the famous *Campbell's Soup Cans* series?
20. What is the name of the famous art museum in Paris?
21. Who is the artist known for creating the sculpture *The Thinker*?
22. What does the term "impressionism" refer to in art?
23. What type of paint did Leonardo da Vinci use for the *Last Supper*?
24. What is the term for the visual balance achieved in a painting?
25. Which artist was known for his "Blue Period"?
26. What Is a triptych?
27. What is the name of the famous art school founded by Walter Gropius?
28. Who created the sculpture of the *Venus de Milo*?
29. What is the difference between a portrait and a landscape painting?
30. Who painted *Girl with a Pearl Earring*?

31. What is the term for art created by pasting various materials onto a surface?
32. Who was the main artist of the Cubist movement?
33. What is the art of making pottery called?
34. Who designed the Guggenheim Museum in New York City?
35. What is the purpose of a vanishing point in art?
36. Which famous street artist is known for his political and social commentary?
37. What is the main feature of Gothic architecture?
38. What is chiaroscuro?
39. Who is considered the father of the Italian Renaissance?
40. What is the term for painting on wet plaster?
41. Who painted the *Birth of Venus*?
42. What does the term "abstract art" mean?
43. Who is the artist behind the famous installation *Infinity Mirrors*?
44. What is a fresco?
45. What is the difference between oil and acrylic paint?
46. Who was the Spanish artist known for his surrealist paintings?
47. What is the term for a large painting applied directly to a wall?

48. What is the main focus of contemporary
    art?
49. Who was the American artist famous for
    her large-scale flower paintings?
50. What is the most famous artwork housed in
    the Louvre Museum?

Chapter 16: Answers

1. Leonardo da Vinci
2. Surrealism
3. Gustave Eiffel
4. Pointillism
5. Michelangelo
6. Salvador Dalí
7. *Salvator Mundi* by Leonardo da Vinci
8. Michelangelo
9. Post-Impressionism
10. Paper
11. Clay
12. Frank Lloyd Wright
13. Calligraphy
14. Acrylic paint
15. Architecture
16. Vincent van Gogh
17. Ikebana
18. Woodcut
19. Andy Warhol
20. The Louvre
21. Auguste Rodin
22. Capturing light and movement
23. Tempera
24. Symmetry
25. Pablo Picasso
26. A three-panelled painting
27. Bauhaus

28. Unknown (classical Greek sculpture)
29. Portrait: a depiction of a person; Landscape:
    a depiction of scenery
30. Johannes Vermeer
31. Collage
32. Pablo Picasso
33. Ceramics
34. Frank Lloyd Wright
35. To create perspective
36. Banksy
37. Pointed arches and ribbed vaults
38. The use of light and shadow
39. Leonardo da Vinci
40. Fresco
41. Sandro Botticelli
42. Art that does not depict recognisable
    scenes or objects
43. Yayoi Kusama
44. A painting on wet plaster
45. Oil takes longer to dry, acrylic dries quickly
46. Salvador Dalí
47. Mural
48. Modern themes and techniques
49. Georgia O'Keeffe
50. *Mona Lisa*

Chapter 17: Animals & Wildlife

1. What is the fastest land animal in the world?
2. What is the largest species of shark?
3. Which bird is known for its ability to mimic human speech?
4. What is the only mammal capable of true flight?
5. What is a baby kangaroo called?
6. Which animal is known as the "King of the Jungle"?
7. What is the tallest animal in the world?
8. Which marine mammal is known for its distinctive tusks?
9. What type of animal is a Komodo dragon?
10. Which bird lays the largest eggs?
11. What is the most venomous snake in the world?
12. What is a group of lions called?
13. Which animal is the largest living primate?
14. What is the name of the largest freshwater fish?
15. What is the national bird of the United States?
16. Which animal can change its colour to blend in with its surroundings?
17. What is the only continent where you can find penguins in the wild?

18. Which insect is known for its ability to carry
    many times its own body weight?
19. What is the longest-living land animal?
20. Which animal has the longest migration of
    any mammal?
21. What type of animal is a platypus?
22. Which bird is known for its elaborate
    courtship dance?
23. What is the collective name for a group of
    crows?
24. Which animal has the strongest bite force
    of any living creature?
25. What is the primary diet of a panda?
26. Which sea creature has three hearts?
27. What is the fastest bird in the world?
28. Which mammal spends almost all of its life
    hanging upside down?
29. What is the largest species of cat?
30. Which animal is known as the "Ship of the
    Desert"?
31. What is the most intelligent species of bird?
32. Which animal is known to sleep standing
    up?
33. What is the largest animal on Earth?
34. Which reptile can live for over 150 years?
35. What type of animal is a fennec?
36. Which mammal is capable of echolocation?
37. What is a group of flamingos called?

38. Which fish is known for being able to generate electric shocks?

39. What is the most common species of owl in the UK?

40. What is the only marsupial native to North America?

41. Which animal has a tongue longer than its body?

42. What type of animal is a binturong, also known as a bearcat?

43. Which bird is the national symbol of New Zealand?

44. What is the smallest mammal in the world?

45. Which animal is famous for playing dead as a defense mechanism?

46. What is the name of the largest land carnivore?

47. Which animal can sleep with one half of its brain at a time?

48. What is the only bird known to fly backwards?

49. Which amphibian can regenerate its limbs?

50. What is the name of the largest species of deer?

Chapter 17: Answers

1. Cheetah
2. Whale shark
3. Parrot
4. Bat
5. Joey
6. Lion
7. Giraffe
8. Walrus
9. Lizard (monitor lizard)
10. Ostrich
11. Inland taipan
12. Pride
13. Gorilla
14. Beluga sturgeon
15. Bald eagle
16. Chameleon
17. Antarctica
18. Ant
19. Galápagos tortoise
20. Gray whale
21. Mammal (specifically, monotreme)
22. Bird of paradise
23. Murder
24. Saltwater crocodile
25. Bamboo
26. Octopus
27. Peregrine falcon

28. Sloth
29. Siberian tiger
30. Camel
31. Crow (New Caledonian crow)
32. Horse
33. Blue whale
34. Tortoise (Galápagos tortoise)
35. Fennec fox
36. Bat
37. Flamboyance
38. Electric eel
39. Barn owl
40. Opossum
41. Chameleon
42. Civet (related to a bearcat)
43. Kiwi
44. Etruscan shrew
45. Opossum
46. Polar bear
47. Dolphin
48. Hummingbird
49. Salamander (axolotl)
50. Moose

Chapter 18: Space & Astronomy

1. What is the closest planet to the Sun?
2. Who was the first person to walk on the Moon?
3. What is the largest planet in our Solar System?
4. What is the name of the galaxy we live in?
5. Which planet is known as the Red Planet?
6. What is the name of the first artificial satellite launched into space?
7. Which planet has the most moons?
8. What is the term for a star that suddenly increases in brightness?
9. Who was the first woman in space?
10. What is the name of the telescope launched into space in 1990?
11. What is the smallest planet in our Solar System?
12. What is the name of the closest star to Earth?
13. Which planet is known for its rings?
14. What is the hottest planet in our Solar System?
15. What is a light-year a measure of?
16. Which planet has a day longer than its year?
17. Who was the first person to travel into space?
18. What is the main element found in the Sun?

19. What is the name of the dwarf planet that was once considered the ninth planet?
20. What is the name of the largest moon of Jupiter?
21. Which planet is known as the "Evening Star"?
22. What is the name of the boundary that marks the edge of the Solar System?
23. What is the term for a rocky object that orbits the Sun but is too small to be a planet?
24. What is the largest type of star called?
25. Which planet has the fastest rotation?
26. What is the name of the rover that landed on Mars in 2021?
27. What is the brightest star in the night sky?
28. What is the name of the force that keeps planets in orbit around the Sun?
29. Which planet is tipped on its side and has a unique rotation?
30. What is the name of the largest volcano in the Solar System?
31. What is the term for a group of stars that forms a recognisable pattern?
32. Who discovered the law of universal gravitation?
33. What is the name of the first spacecraft to leave the Solar System?
34. What is a black hole?

35. What phenomenon causes the Northern Lights?
36. Which planet is known as Earth's twin?
37. What is the name of the first animal sent into space?
38. Which planet is named after the Roman god of the sea?
39. What is a comet's tail made of?
40. What is the name of the galaxy closest to the Milky Way?
41. What is the process by which stars generate energy?
42. What is the name of the space station currently orbiting Earth?
43. What is a supernova?
44. Which planet is known for its Great Red Spot?
45. What is the name of the spacecraft that explored Pluto in 2015?
46. What is the term for the dark patches seen on the surface of the Moon?
47. What is the name of the boundary between the Earth's atmosphere and outer space?
48. Which planet has the largest canyon in the Solar System?
49. What is the approximate age of the universe?
50. What is the name of the current Mars mission by NASA?

Chapter 18: Answers

1. Mercury
2. Neil Armstrong
3. Jupiter
4. Milky Way
5. Mars
6. Sputnik 1
7. Jupiter
8. Nova
9. Valentina Tereshkova
10. Hubble Space Telescope
11. Mercury
12. Proxima Centauri
13. Saturn
14. Venus
15. Distance light travels in one year
16. Venus
17. Yuri Gagarin
18. Hydrogen
19. Pluto
20. Ganymede
21. Venus
22. Heliopause
23. Asteroid
24. Red supergiant
25. Jupiter
26. Perseverance
27. Sirius

28. Gravity
29. Uranus
30. Olympus Mons
31. Constellation
32. Isaac Newton
33. Voyager 1
34. Collapsed star with intense gravitational pull
35. Solar wind (charged particles from the Sun)
36. Venus
37. Laika (a dog)
38. Neptune
39. Gas and dust particles
40. Andromeda Galaxy
41. Nuclear fusion
42. International Space Station (ISS)
43. Exploding star
44. Jupiter
45. New Horizons
46. Maria
47. Kármán line
48. Mars (Valles Marineris)
49. 13.8 billion years
50. Mars 2020 (Perseverance rover)

Chapter 19: Famous Inventions & Discoveries

1. Which invention, patented by Johannes Gutenberg, revolutionised the spread of knowledge in Europe?
2. What did Alexander Fleming discover in 1928?
3. Who is credited with inventing the airplane?
4. What is the name of the first antibiotic discovered?
5. Who invented the printing press?
6. What was the first vaccine ever created?
7. Who discovered the theory of relativity?
8. What invention is Thomas Edison best known for?
9. Who invented the World Wide Web?
10. What was Alfred Nobel's most famous invention?
11. Who discovered penicillin?
12. What is the name of the first man-made satellite?
13. Who invented the first practical light bulb?
14. Who invented the steam engine?
15. What is the name of the machine that revolutionised the textile industry?
16. Who discovered the circulation of blood?

17. What was the first element discovered using a spectroscope?
18. Who is known as the father of modern physics?
19. What did Marie Curie discover?
20. Who invented the phonograph?
21. What was the first plastic material invented?
22. Who discovered the structure of DNA?
23. Who invented the electric motor?
24. What did James Watt improve to help spark the Industrial Revolution?
25. Who invented the first windshield wiper, which was initially designed for streetcars?
26. Who discovered the first law of thermodynamics?
27. What was the first mechanical computer called?
28. Who invented the microwave oven?
29. What is the name of the first artificial heart implant?
30. Who discovered radioactivity?
31. What did Henry Ford invent to revolutionise manufacturing?
32. Who invented the barometer?
33. What was the first spacecraft to land on the Moon?
34. Who invented the television?
35. Who discovered the laws of motion?

36. What was the first chemical element discovered?
37. Who invented the safety pin?
38. Who invented the first successful airplane?
39. What did Isaac Newton invent to measure time accurately?
40. Who discovered the planet Uranus?
41. What did Galileo invent to observe the stars?
42. Who invented the first digital computer?
43. What is the name of the first cloned animal?
44. Who invented the first practical electric battery?
45. What did John Logie Baird invent?
46. Who discovered the X-ray?
47. What is the name of the first mass-produced car?
48. Who invented the sewing machine?
49. What is considered the first written language?
50. Who invented the first camera?

Chapter 19: Answers

1. The Printing Press
2. Penicillin
3. The Wright brothers (Orville and Wilbur Wright)
4. Penicillin
5. Johannes Gutenberg
6. Smallpox vaccine
7. Albert Einstein
8. The light bulb
9. Tim Berners-Lee
10. Dynamite
11. Alexander Fleming
12. Sputnik 1
13. Thomas Edison
14. James Watt
15. Spinning Jenny
16. William Harvey
17. Cesium (spectroscopy)
18. Albert Einstein
19. Radium and polonium
20. Thomas Edison
21. Bakelite
22. James Watson and Francis Crick
23. Michael Faraday
24. The steam engine
25. Mary Anderson
26. Joule

27. Difference Engine (by Charles Babbage)
28. Percy Spencer
29. Jarvik-7
30. Henri Becquerel (with Marie Curie)
31. Assembly line
32. Evangelista Torricelli
33. Apollo 11 Lunar Module (Eagle)
34. Philo Farnsworth
35. Isaac Newton
36. Phosphorus
37. Walter Hunt
38. The Wright brothers
39. Pendulum clock
40. William Herschel
41. Telescope
42. Alan Turing (with contributions from others)
43. Dolly the sheep
44. Alessandro Volta
45. Television
46. Wilhelm Conrad Roentgen
47. Ford Model T
48. Elias Howe
49. Cuneiform (Sumerians)
50. Nicéphore Niépce

Chapter 20: World Festivals & Traditions

1. In which country is the festival of Diwali celebrated?
2. What is the main tradition of Thanksgiving in the United States?
3. Where is the Running of the Bulls festival held?
4. What does the Chinese New Year celebrate?
5. What is the famous German beer festival called?
6. Which country is known for its Carnival celebrations?
7. What is the name of the Hindu spring festival of colours?
8. In which country is the Day of the Dead celebrated?
9. What is the main food eaten during Hanukkah?
10. What is the tradition of burning an effigy on Guy Fawkes Night in the UK?
11. Where is the festival of La Tomatina held?
12. What is the main religious holiday in Christianity?
13. What is the name of the Japanese festival that celebrates cherry blossoms?

14. In which country is the festival of Eid al-Fitr celebrated?

15. What is the main event of Rio Carnival?

16. What tradition involves singing carols during Christmas?

17. What is the name of the lantern festival in Thailand?

18. In which country is Oktoberfest held?

19. What do people celebrate on Bastille Day in France?

20. What is the name of the ancient Celtic festival that marks the end of the harvest season?

21. Where is the Edinburgh Fringe Festival held?

22. What is the main purpose of Ramadan in Islam?

23. Which festival is known for the lighting of the menorah?

24. What is the main dance performed at Hawaiian luaus?

25. Where is the Holi festival celebrated?

26. What do people in Spain traditionally eat on New Year's Eve?

27. What is the main event of the Rio de Janeiro Carnival?

28. What is the traditional Scottish celebration on New Year's Eve?

29. What do people celebrate on St. Patrick's Day?
30. What is the traditional attire worn during Oktoberfest?
31. What do people in India celebrate during the festival of Raksha Bandhan?
32. What is the main tradition of Easter?
33. In which country is the Midsummer festival celebrated?
34. What is the main tradition of the Jewish festival of Purim?
35. What is the name of the dragon boat festival in China?
36. Where is the Burning Man festival held?
37. What is the main event of the Notting Hill Carnival?
38. What is the traditional Japanese tea ceremony called?
39. What is the name of the harvest festival celebrated in the UK?
40. What is the main food eaten during Passover?
41. Where is the Sundance Film Festival held?
42. What is the main event of the Mardi Gras festival?
43. What is the main theme of the Dia de los Muertos festival?
44. Where is the Festival of San Fermin held?

45. What do people celebrate on International Women's Day?
46. What is the main event of the Coachella Music Festival?
47. What is the significance of the Lunar New Year?
48. What is the traditional Swedish Christmas drink?
49. What do people throw during the Holi festival?
50. What is the main event of the Cannes Film Festival?

Chapter 20: Answers

1. India
2. Eating a traditional Thanksgiving meal (usually turkey)
3. Spain (Pamplona)
4. Lunar New Year celebrations and family reunions
5. Oktoberfest
6. Brazil
7. Holi
8. Mexico
9. Latkes (potato pancakes)
10. Bonfire Night (burning the Guy)
11. Buñol, Spain
12. Christmas
13. Hanami
14. Worldwide (Muslim communities)
15. Samba parade
16. Singing Christmas carols
17. Yi Peng (Lantern Festival)
18. Germany
19. French Revolution (Storming of the Bastille)
20. Samhain
21. Edinburgh, Scotland
22. Fasting from dawn to sunset
23. Hanukkah
24. Hula dance
25. India

26.12 grapes for good luck
27.Samba parades and street parties
28.Hogmanay
29.Irish heritage and culture (St. Patrick's Day)
30.Lederhosen and dirndl
31.Celebrating the bond between brothers and sisters
32.Easter egg hunts
33.Sweden
34.Wearing costumes and giving gifts
35.Dragon Boat Festival
36.Nevada, USA
37.Street parades and music
38.Chanoyu
39.Harvest Festival
40.Matzah (unleavened bread)
41.Utah, USA
42.Parades and bead throwing
43.Honouring deceased loved ones
44.Pamplona, Spain
45.Women's achievements and rights
46.Music performances and art installations
47.Celebrating the new lunar year and family gatherings
48.Glögg
49.Coloured powders (gulal)
50.Film screenings and awards presentations